JOE WILKINSON
MY AUTOBIOGRAPHY

WWW.PENGUIN.CO.UK

ALSO BY JOE WILKINSON

THE BEGINNER'S GUIDE TO ARMED SCRUMPING

THE COOK, THE THIEF, THE WIFE AND HER NIT NURSE

HOW TO GET AHEAD IN BUSINESS
(DON'T PUT YOUR FIST IN YOUR MOUTH)

TRAINSPOTTER SPOTTER'S LOG BOOK: AN ENTHUSIAST'S RECORD
OF NAMES AND THEIR PARKA JACKETS

THE 12 STEPS OF AAA (ALIENS' ALCOHOLICS ANONYMOUS)

THE JOY OF SEX WITH DINNER LADIES

HOW TO BE A HAPPY MUM (CO-WRITTEN WITH THE 1975
WOLVERHAMPTON WANDERERS FOOTBALL TEAM)

FIBREGLASS AND COMPOSITE MATERIALS: A GUIDE
TO HIGH-PERFORMANCE NON-METALLIC MATERIALS

JOE AND THE BOG-STANDARD CHOCOLATE FACTORY

THE DOS AND DON'TS OF CLONING YOURSELF
(PAMPHLET)

JOE WILKINSON
MY AUTOBIOGRAPHY
ILLUSTRATED BY HENRY PAKER

bantam

TRANSWORLD PUBLISHERS
PENGUIN RANDOM HOUSE, ONE EMBASSY GARDENS, 8 VIADUCT GARDENS,
LONDON SW11 7BW
WWW.PENGUIN.CO.UK

TRANSWORLD IS PART OF THE PENGUIN RANDOM HOUSE GROUP OF COMPANIES
WHOSE ADDRESSES CAN BE FOUND AT GLOBAL.PENGUINRANDOMHOUSE.COM

FIRST PUBLISHED IN GREAT BRITAIN IN 2023 BY BANTAM
AN IMPRINT OF TRANSWORLD PUBLISHERS

TEXT © THE JOE WILKINSON COMPANY LTD 2023
ILLUSTRATIONS © HENRY PAKER 2023

JOE WILKINSON HAS ASSERTED HIS RIGHT UNDER THE COPYRIGHT,
DESIGNS AND PATENTS ACT 1988 TO BE IDENTIFIED AS THE AUTHOR OF THIS WORK.

A CIP CATALOGUE RECORD FOR THIS BOOK
IS AVAILABLE FROM THE BRITISH LIBRARY.

ISBN 9781787630819

TYPESET IN BACK ISSUES 9PT BY HENRY PAKER
PRINTED IN ITALY.

THE AUTHORIZED REPRESENTATIVE IN THE EEA IS PENGUIN RANDOM HOUSE IRELAND,
MORRISON CHAMBERS, 32 NASSAU STREET, DUBLIN D02 YH68.

PENGUIN RANDOM HOUSE IS COMMITTED TO A SUSTAINABLE
FUTURE FOR OUR BUSINESS, OUR READERS AND OUR PLANET.
THIS BOOK IS MADE FROM FOREST STEWARDSHIP COUNCIL® CERTIFIED PAPER.

THIS BOOK IS DEDICATED
TO MY EIGHTEEN ALSATIANS.

DRAGØR
MINTY
FOXY LADY
THE ANGLE GRINDER
RITA
SUE
BOB
MIKE PATTERSON
TURPS
BATTERY ACID
BIG VAL
MERTHYR TYDFIL
LUCIFER
GUNPOWDER
BERNIE NOLAN
DASHER
COURTNEY
THE MUSCLES FROM BRUSSELS

...YOU COMPLETE ME

CONTENTS (OF MY FRIDGE)

MARGARINE

CONTENTS (OF MY BOOK)

PROLOGUE

I DON'T KNOW WHAT A PROLOGUE IS, SO INSTEAD I'VE
STUCK IN THE CRAWLEY/REDHILL BUS TIMETABLE.

420 / 460

Crawley/Redhill - Reigate - Tadworth - Epsom/Sutton

420: Crawley – Gatwick – Whitebushes – East Surrey Hospital – Redhill – Reigate – Lower Kingswood – Tadworth – Preston – Banstead – Belmont – Sutton – Sutton Bus Garage

460: Crawley – Gatwick – Whitebushes – East Surrey Hospital – Redhill – Reigate – Lower Kingswood – Walton-on-the-Hill – Tadworth – Preston – Tattenham Corner – Epsom

Talking bus

Daily from 16th January 2021
Inc. journeys on Service 820 Mon-Fri only

Mondays to Fridays

Service	460	460	420	460	420	460	460	420	460	420	420	460	420	460	420	460	420	460
Crawley Bus Station Stop I						0601		0645				0749		0901		1001		
Gatwick Road North						0609		0654				0758		0910		1010		
Gatwick South Terminal	0450	0532		0548		0613	0630	0658				0803		0915		1015		
Horley Lumley Road, A23	0454	0536		0552		0618	0635	0703				0808		0920		1020		
Salfords Church	0458	0540		0556		0623	0640	0709				0814		0926		1026		
Whitebushes Spencer Way	0503	0545		0601		0629	0646	0716				0821	0902	0933	1002	1033	1102	
East Surrey Hospital	0505	0547		0603		0631	0648	0719				0824	0904	0936	1004	1036	1104	
Redhill Bus Station (arr)	0512	0554		0610		0638	0655	0727				0834	0912	0945	1012	1045	1112	
Redhill Bus Station (dep)	0514	0556	0558	0612		0641	0658	0703	0731		0812	0838	0916	0949	1016	1049	1116	
Reigate Bell Street	0521	0604	0606	0620	0647	0650	0708	0713	0743		0827	0850	0928	1001	1028	1101	1128	1143
Lower Kingswood Fox	0529	0612	0615	0629	0656	0659	0718b	0725	0753b		0842	0901b	0938	1011	1038	1111	1138	1153b
Walton Oaks (see note 'b')	↓	↓	↓			0729		0805	0813		↓	0911		↓		1121	↓	1200
Walton-on-the-Hill Howard Close	↓	↓	↓	0638			0809		0915			1021		↓		1206		
Tadworth Station	0535	0619	0622	0643	0706	0709	0737	0739	0815	0819	0852	0921	0946	1027	1046	1127	1146	1206
Merland Rise Sports Centre		0625		0710	↓	0746		0823	0856		0950		1050		1150	↓		
Marbles Way, Merefield Gardens	0541	0625	↓	0649	↓	0715	0743		0821	↓		0927		1033		1133	↓	1212
Tattenham Corner Station	0545	0630	↓	0654		0720	0748		0826	↓		0932		1038		1138	↓	1217
Epsom High Street Stop K	0553	0638	↓	0703	↓	0729	0757		0835	↓		0941		1047		1147	↓	1226
Tattenham Way Reigate Road			0610		0716		0753		0829	0902		0956		1056		1156		
Banstead Marks & Spencer			0635		0722		0759		0835	0908		1002		1102		1202		
Belmont Downs Road			0640		0728		0805		0841	0914		1008		1108		1208		
Sutton Station			0644		0734		0811		0847	0920		1014		1114		1214		
Sutton Bus Garage			0649							0926		1020		1120		1220		

Mondays to Fridays cont...

Service	460	820	420	460	420	460	420	460	420	820	460	420	460	420	460	420	460	460
Crawley Bus Stn, Stop I	1101			1201		1305		1408			1513		1621		1730		1830	
Gatwick Road North	1110			1210		1314		1417			1522		1630		1739		1839	
Gatwick South Terminal	1115			1215		1319		1422			1527		1635		1744		1844	
Horley Lumley Road, A23	1120			1220		1324		1427			1532		1640		1749		1849	
Salfords Church	1126			1226		1330		1433			1538		1646		1755		1854	
Whitebushes Spencer Way	1133		1202	1233	1302	1337	1402	1440	1509		1545	1616	1653	1731	1802	1833	1900	
East Surrey Hospital	1136		1204	1236	1304	1340	1404	1443	1511		1548	1618	1656	1733	1805	1835	1902	
Redhill Bus Station (arr)	1145		1212	1245	1312	1349	1412	1452	1519		1557	1626	1706	1741	1814	1844	1912	
Redhill Bus Station (dep)	1149		1216	1249	1316	1353	1416	1457	1524	1551	1602	1630	1711	1746	1818	1848	1916	1934
Reigate Bell Street	1201		1228	1301	1328	1405	1428	1509	1536	1603	1614	1642	1723	1758	1830	1859	1926	1943
Lower Kingswood Fox	1211		1238	1311	1338	1415	1438	1519	1546b	1613	1624b	1654b		1733b	1810b	1842	1909	1934	1951
Walton Oaks (see note b)	↓	1248							1555	1630*	1633	1703	1730	1743	1819			
Walton-on-the-Hill Howard Cl.	1221	y		1321		1425		1529		1623	1637		1747		1850		1943	
Tadworth Station	1227		1246	1327	1346	1431	1446	1535	1601	y	1643	1710	1736	1753	1826	1855	1916	1948	1958
Merland Rise Sports Centre	↓		1250	↓	1350	↓	1450		1605	↓		1714	1740	↓	1830		1920	
Marbles Way, Merefield Gdns.	1233	↓		1333		1437		1541		↓	1649		1759		1900		1953	2003
Tattenham Corner Stn.	1238	↓		1338		1442		1546		↓	1654		1803		1904		1957	2007
Epsom High Street, Stop K	1247	↓		1347		1451		1555		↓	1703		1812		1911		2004	2013
Tattenham Way Reigate Rd.		↓	1256		1356		1456		1611	↓		1720	1745		1835		1924	
Banstead Marks & Spencer		1300	1302		1402		1502		1617	1645		1726	1752		1840		1929	
Belmont Downs Road		1306	1308		1408		1508		1623	1651		1732	1758		1846		1934	
Sutton Station		1311	1314		1414		1514		1628	1657		1738	1804		1852		1939	
Sutton Bus Garage			1320		1420		1520		1634			1744	1809		1857		1944	

CODE: ○ Rail Station nearby. **SDO** Schooldays only. (**NSD** Non-Schooldays) y Via A217 Burgh Heath.
b Does not serve the Mill Road bus stop, or the Tadworth Court, Tadorne Road and The Lye bus stops on Tadworth Street. * 820 serves Walton Oaks after Walton-on-the-Hill.

Partly supported by SURREY

9

INTRODUCTION

I MUST REMEMBER TO FILL THIS BIT OUT, AND FOR
SHIT'S SAKE DON'T SWEAR ON THE FIRST PAGE.

THIS IS ME

I USED TO LIVE OVER THE HILL FROM THE WORLD'S ONLY RUDE FELL WALKER.

MORNING!

FXXK OFF.

I LIKE YOUR NEW SCARF.

FXXK OFF.

I AM NOT A TRAINSPOTTER. NOTHING COULD BE FURTHER FROM THE TRUTH.

I AM IN FACT A TRAINSPOTTER SPOTTER.

CLICK

WHEN I SPOT A TRAINSPOTTER I HAVEN'T SPOTTED BEFORE I MARK THEM DOWN IN THIS SPECIAL BOOK FOR TRAINSPOTTER SPOTTERS.

IT HAS ALL THE UK'S TRAINSPOTTERS IN IT. WHEN YOU SPOT A TRAINSPOTTER YOU UNDERLINE THEM AND I LIKE TO ALSO JOT DOWN WHERE AND WHEN I SAW THEM AND HOW THEY GOT THE STAIN ON THEIR PARKA JACKET.

Name: Paul Turner
Gender: Male
Top Speed: 2.4 mph
Preferred thermos:
470ml Stainless Steel
SuperLight
Hot King 5000

Notes:
- Didcot Parkway
- Thursday
- He bought it pre-stained to save time.

OTHER CATEGORIES IN THE BOOK INCLUDE:
- TRAINSPOTTERS WHO CAN KICK THEMSELVES IN THE FACE
- TRAINSPOTTERS WHO DRINK THE JUICE IN A CAN OF KIDNEY BEANS
- TRAINSPOTTERS WHO LOOK LIKE KIM JONG UN
- TRAINSPOTTERS WHO ARE WAITING TO HAVE A WART FROZEN OFF
- TRAINSPOTTERS WHO ARE PART WEREWOLF
- TRAINSPOTTERS WHO SPEND A GOOD CHUNK OF THEIR TIME
  JUST SITTING IN A LITTLE CHEF MAKING PAPER HATS OUT OF NAPKINS
- TRAINSPOTTERS WHOSE TROUSERS ARE TOO TIGHT SO YOU CAN SEE
  THE CONTOUR OF THEIR NUTS
- TRAINSPOTTERS WITH CONSTANT NOSE BLEEDS
- TRAINSPOTTERS WHO RIDE HORSES SIDE SADDLE

I STARTED RECYCLING IN 1985 WHEN I REALIZED THAT CRISP PACKETS AND TIN CANS MADE EXCELLENT LITTER.

SO NOW, WHENEVER I MOUNT A NEW MOOSE HEAD, I DON'T WANT TO BE ONE OF 'THOSE GUYS' WHO JUST THROWS AWAY THE REST OF THE BODY. IT'S A WASTE OF MOOSE.

SO I ALWAYS KEEP THE OTHER 90% AND MOUNT IT ON THE OTHER SIDE OF THE WALL.

UNFORTUNATELY THE OTHER SIDE IS THE GUPTAS BUT I'M SURE THEY DON'T MIND.

WHEN I'M FLUSH, I BUY AIR BAGS IN BULK AND THEN ATTACH THEM EVERYWHERE.

THERE WAS ONLY ONE PLACE I FORGOT TO PUT ONE.

BALLS.

I WAS ONCE FIRED OUT OF A CANNON BUT I'D PUT ON WEIGHT AGAIN SO THE FRICTION MEANT I JUST SLID OUT VERY SLOWLY.

I HAD TO GAFFER TAPE FOUR MALE SEX DOLLS TOGETHER BECAUSE NOWHERE SELLS MUG TREES ANY MORE.

THE EARLY
DAYS

I WAS RAISED BY WOLVES...

...FOOTBALL CLUB. I WAS LEFT ON THE STEPS OF MOLINEUX STADIUM IN 1975.

MOLINEUX

THESE ARE JUST STRAY DOGS

ASSISTANT MANAGER SAMMY CHUNG INTRODUCED ME TO EVERYONE AT HALF TIME DURING THE SPURS GAME.

I FOUND THIS UGLY BABY OUTSIDE.

THE PLAYERS TOOK TO MOTHERHOOD LIKE A DUCK TO WATER AND EVEN SANG ME TO SLEEP AT NIGHT.

♪ PISS ON THE VILLA
WE'RE GOING TO PISS ON THE VILLA ♪

BUT THE FANS BLAMED ME FOR WOLVES GETTING RELEGATED. PROBABLY BECAUSE, IN THE LIVERPOOL GAME, CENTRE BACK MAURICE DALY PLAYED WHILE PUSHING MY PRAM...

...AND WHEN JOHN TOSHACK BROKE THROUGH MAURICE STRUGGLED TO TRACK BACK. THAT'S WHEN THE CHANTING STARTED...

THE BEARDED BABY IS A WXXKER! THE BEARDED BABY IS A WXXKER!

THEN I LOST MY FAVOURITE TEDDY AND, WHILE THE PLAYERS SEARCHED FOR IT, LIVERPOOL SCORED AGAIN AND WOLVES WENT DOWN.

THE FANS STILL BURN AN EFFIGY OF MR HUGGLESWORTH OUTSIDE THE GROUND ON MATCH DAYS.

I LOVED SCRUMPING. BUT I DIDN'T GO SCRUMPING FOR APPLES. I'D GO SCRUMPING FOR CAR RADIOS.

IF YOU'RE HOLDING A WICKER BASKET IT'S JUST SCRUMPING!

WHICH QUICKLY ESCALATED TO AN ARMED SCRUMPING.

EVERYONE ON THE FLOOR, THIS IS A FXXKING SCRUMPING!

ANY OF YOU FXXKING PRICKS MOVE, AND I'LL SCRUMP EVERY MOTHERFXXKIN' LAST ONE OF YOU!

I WAS LATER HAULED IN TO TAKE PART IN A SCRUMPING LINE-UP.

BUT A COUPLE OF MY SCRUMPING ASSOCIATES NOBBLED THE WITNESS.

IT WAS THE LITTLE GIRL WITH PINK RIBBONS IN HER HAIR.

I WAS EVEN FEATURED IN THE BBC1 *CRIMEWATCH* SPIN-OFF *SCRUMPWATCH* WHEN I WAS CAUGHT ON CCTV RAM-SCRUMPING MY VAN INTO THE FRONT OF DIXONS.

BUT MY GREATEST SCRUMP WAS WHEN I SCRUMPED THE EDVARD MUNCH PAINTING 'THE SCREAM'.

WHICH I GAVE TO THE WOLVERHAMPTON WANDERERS TEAM AS A MOTHER'S DAY PRESENT.

WE SHOULDN'T BE LOSING TO THAT PILE OF SHIT.

I DON'T WANT TO SHOW OFF BUT I CONSISTENTLY HAD THE MOST NITS AT SCHOOL...

THEY'LL GIVE THEM A PRIZE FOR ANY OLD...

PRIZE DAY

I VISITED THE NIT NURSE SO OFTEN THAT WE WOULD FINISH EACH OTHER'S SENTENCES.

I'VE CHECKED YOUR SCALP AND YOU'VE GOT...

...WHAT IT TAKES TO MAKE IT IN THIS BUSINESS WE CALL 'SHOW'?

NO, NITS AGAIN.

YOU HAVE TO STOP...

... AND SMELL THE ROSES SOMETIMES.

NO, RUBBING YOUR HEAD ON STRAY DOGS.

AND WHY DO YOU TELL EVERYONE THAT WE FINISH EACH OTHER'S...

JIGSAWS.

AT SCHOOL WE HAD TO DO WORK EXPERIENCE AND I WAS SHIPPED OFF TO A MAXIMUM SECURITY PRISON IN WEST TEXAS...

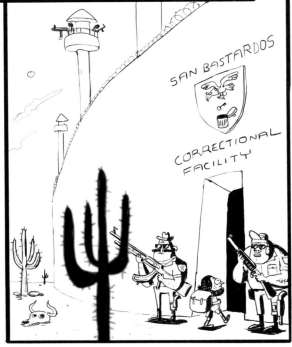

I WOULD BE WORKING ON DEATH ROW, PREPARING THE CONDEMNED MEN THEIR LAST MEAL.

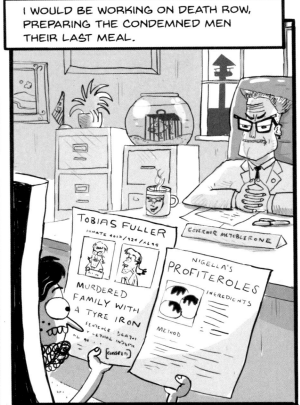

THE ATMOSPHERE WAS PRETTY GRIM...

AND UNFORTUNATELY I DROPPED THE BALL WITH TOBIAS'S PROFITEROLES.

I ASKED HIM IF HE WOULDN'T MIND FILLING IN ONE OF THE ASSESSMENT FORMS I'D BEEN GIVEN BUT HE DIDN'T ANSWER.

I EXPLAINED THIS COULD AFFECT MY CHANCES OF GETTING INTO SIXTH FORM COLLEGE, BUT IT WAS LIKE HE DIDN'T CARE.

BUT THINGS PICKED UP WHEN THE LADS LET ME PRESS THE BUTTON THAT SET IN MOTION HIS LETHAL INJECTION.

IT WAS LATER PROVED THAT HE COULDN'T HAVE COMMITTED THOSE MURDERS SO THAT WILL HAUNT ME FOR EVER. BUT I GUESS THAT'S WHAT WORK EXPERIENCE IS ALL ABOUT.

GROWING UP I DIDN'T HAVE AN IMAGINARY FRIEND... I HAD AN IMAGINARY AIR TRAFFIC CONTROLLER.

BUT BECAUSE OF THE STRESS OF HIS WORK, HE'D DRINK A LOT AND THAT'S NOT GREAT FOR A KID TO BE AROUND.

AND HE WOULD GET QUITE MOROSE WHEN HE WAS DRUNK SO WE LOST TOUCH.

AHHH FXXK AEROPLANES!

BUT I DO WONDER WHAT BECAME OF HIM. I IMAGINE HE HAD A HEART ATTACK BEHIND A WHEELIE BIN BUT I GUESS WE'LL NEVER KNOW.

THE THING I REGRET MOST FROM MY YOUTH IS THROWING A TURD INTO A TORNADO.

SORRY, I DIDN'T THINK THAT THROUGH.

WHAT WAS MOST DISAPPOINTING WAS THAT I LIVED UP TO MY SCHOOL YEARBOOK QUOTE.

JOE WILKINSON
Most likely to cover the entire town in his own shit.

JOE WILKINSON
Most likely to cover the
entire town in his own shit.

TIM O'SULLIVAN
Most likely to be able
to replace a roof tile
without using a ladder.

BARBARA KNELL
Most likely to be
buried in a
Y-shaped coffin.

RAJ HASELTINE
Most likely to
wear a monocle.

ZURGFNÆËL-JŌXXX/974
Most likely to one day
return to his home planet.

GEMIMA SAUNDERS
Most likely to get
hit by a bus.

MORRIS MORTON
Most likely to be
mistaken for
Marcel Morton.

MARCEL MORTON
Most likely to be
mistaken for
Morris Morton.

SIMON SMITH
Most likely to
go completely bald.

KIM JONG UN
Most likely to take over his dad's business.

DAVID STOKES
Most likely to be wrongly accused of being 'a bit handsy'.

IAN GLOCK
Most likely to be bothered by ducks.

GARY WILMER
Most likely to be buried in a G-shaped coffin.

ROY HENNING
Least likely to be able to replace a roof tile without using a ladder.

SARIKA CHOPRA
Most likely to make you feel a bit sleepy.

ARCHIBALD STAPLEY
Most likely to be asked to repeat Year 5 (again).

COLIN CREASEY
Most likely to be a London cab driver.

FLOELLA DAVIS
Most likely to get lost on the way to the photographer's.

THEN I GOT SOME NEWS THAT SHOOK MY WORLD.

WE'RE NOT YOUR REAL MUM.

SO I STARTED LOOKING INTO MY FAMILY TREE. TURNS OUT MY GREAT-GRANDAD INVENTED THE TOFFEE APPLE...

HE'S GOT MY HIGH CHEEKBONES!

APPARENTLY ONE DAY HE DECIDED TO COVER AN APPLE IN TOFFEE. BUT HE ALSO COVERED HIS HAT IN TOFFEE. AND HIS UMBRELLA.

AND HIS FURNITURE.

HE COVERED EVERYTHING IN TOFFEE BECAUSE HE WAS MAD. THE TOFFEE APPLE WAS JUST A HAPPY ACCIDENT.

THE
DATING SCENE

BUT I'VE ALWAYS BEEN ABLE TO CHAT UP WOMEN WHO ARE PART FISH.

ARE YOU A MERMAID?

WOULD YOU LIKE TO GO TO THE CINEMA WITH ME?

YES.

YES.

CAN I THROW MY DRINK OVER YOU SO YOU TURN INTO A MERMAID?

I'D RATHER YOU DIDN'T.

SPLASH

BUT I FLIRTATIOUSLY DID IT ANYWAY.

IT TURNED OUT SHE WAS A RARE TYPE OF MERMAID THAT IS A MASSIVE TROUT FROM THE WAIST UP.

EXCUSE ME, I CAN'T SEE, YOUR HEAD'S IN THE WAY.

THIS IS WHY I DIDN'T WANT YOU TO DO IT.

I GET THAT NOW.

THEN I THOUGHT I'D GO ON A DOUBLE DATE BUT
I COULDN'T FIND THREE OTHER PEOPLE TO GO WITH ME.

WORKING
FOR THE MAN

I GOT A JOB WORKING IN THE LOUVRE ART GALLERY...

HER EYES REALLY DO FOLLOW YOU AROUND THE ROOM DON'T THEY?

...BEING THE MONA LISA'S WANDERING EYES.

SHE'S GOT VERY BEADY EYES HASN'T SHE?

FXXK YOU!

JOE, CAN I HAVE A WORD IN MY OFFICE?

THEN I GOT A JOB HAMMERING IN THE 'DANGER CLIFF EDGE' SIGNS.

I ALSO WORKED AS A MOTORCYCLE STUNTMAN BUT I COULD NEVER NAIL THE LANDING.

I DIDN'T LISTEN ON THE FIRST DAY OF PILOT SCHOOL AND PLOUGHED A 747 AT A MOUNTAIN.

NO ONE KNOWS HOW THEY'RE GOING TO REACT WHEN FACED WITH THEIR OWN DEMISE.

DON'T PEE ON THE CONTROL PANELS!!

WHY NOT? WE'RE GOING TO DIE ANYWAY!

SO WHEN THE INSTRUCTOR LEVELLED THE PLANE OFF, I FELT LIKE A RIGHT PRAT...

LET ME CLEAN THAT UP FOR YOU.

I FELT LIKE AN EVEN BIGGER PRAT WHEN I REMEMBERED WE WERE ONLY IN A SIMULATOR.

BLIMEY, THOSE THINGS ARE REALISTIC.

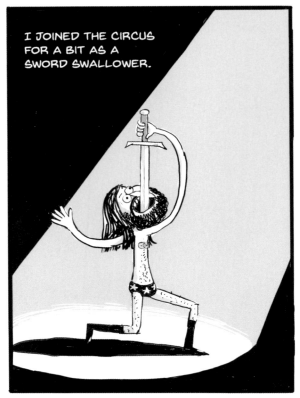

I JOINED THE CIRCUS FOR A BIT AS A SWORD SWALLOWER.

BUT NO ONE TOLD ME YOU WEREN'T SUPPOSED TO SWALLOW THE WHOLE THING.

YOU'RE MEANT TO KEEP THE HANDLE STICKING OUT SO YOU CAN PULL IT OUT AGAIN.

OH I SEE. I THINK I'LL HAVE TO NIP DOWN TO BOOTS.

I'LL RUN YOU DOWN THERE.

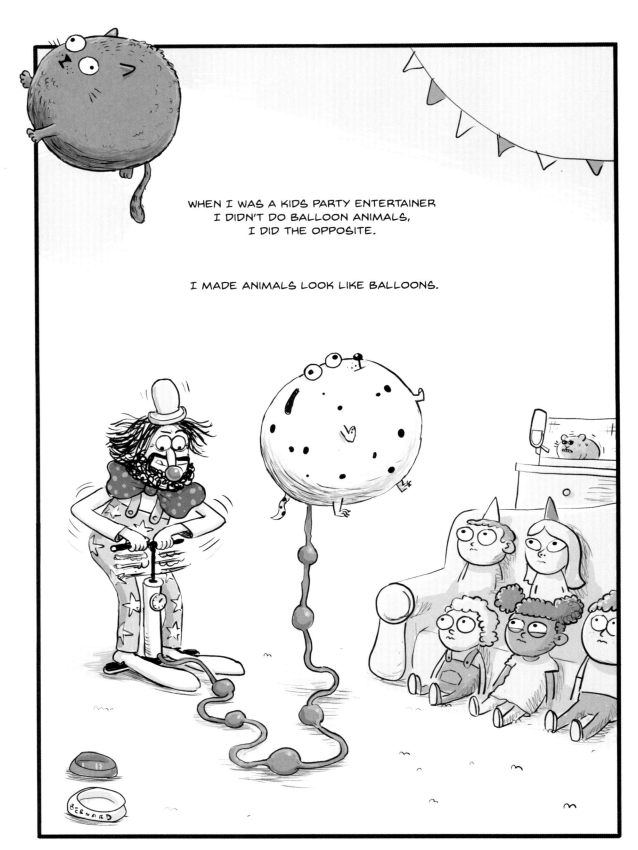

WHEN I WAS A KIDS PARTY ENTERTAINER
I DIDN'T DO BALLOON ANIMALS,
I DID THE OPPOSITE.

I MADE ANIMALS LOOK LIKE BALLOONS.

FOR A WHILE I WORKED AS A WEDDING PHOTOGRAPHER BUT I SPECIALIZED IN TAKING PICTURES OF JILTED BRIDES.

YOU LOOK BEAUTIFUL ...CONSIDERING.

I'D GET THEM TO POSE FOR ALL THE SAME PICTURES, THE ONLY DIFFERENCE BEING SHE WAS ON HER TOD...

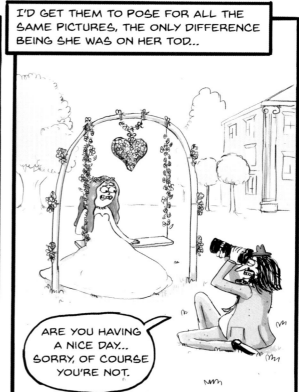

ARE YOU HAVING A NICE DAY... SORRY, OF COURSE YOU'RE NOT.

NOW GAZE INTO WHERE HIS EYES WOULD HAVE BEEN.

HOW ABOUT A PICCY WITH THE GROOM'S FAMILY? OK MAYBE NOT...

ALTHOUGH I LIED ON MY CV THAT I WAS AN EXPERIENCED SUBMARINE CAPTAIN.

THAT WAS SOON REVEALED TO BE A FIB WHEN I HUNG A PICTURE OF MY FAVOURITE ACTOR, LOU DIAMOND PHILLIPS, ON THE WALL.

SORRY GUYS, NEXT TIME I'LL USE BLU TACK.

I DON'T WANT TO SOUND LIKE I'M SHOWING OFF BUT I DO A HELL OF A LOT OF TEMP WORK...

YOU CAN ALWAYS TELL THE JOB'S NOT GOING THAT WELL WHEN HR HAND YOU A LIST OF THINGS THEY'D RATHER YOU DIDN'T SNIFF ANY MORE.

Please stop sniffing:

-Tipp-Ex
-marker pens
-people in accounts

MY ARGUMENT IS ALWAYS IF THEY DON'T WANT ME TO SNIFF THEM THEY SHOULDN'T WEAR LYNX AFRICA.

ONCE AGAIN I WAS GIVEN AN OFFICIAL WARNING BUT THIS TIME I WASN'T HAVING IT.

SHOW ME WHERE IT SAYS IN MY CONTRACT THAT I CAN'T SNIFF MY CO-WORKERS.

BUT HR WERE ADAMANT, SO I TOOK IT TO MY LINE MANAGER.

I DON'T KNOW IF YOU KNOW THIS, BUT RICHARD BRANSON OWNS ALL THE COMPANIES IN THE WORLD (EXCEPT FOR A KEY CUTTER'S IN FROME).

AND THE MANNEQUIN FACTORY I WAS WORKING IN WAS NO EXCEPTION.

SO I CONSTRUCTED A RAFT OUT OF MANNEQUIN PARTS AND AN OLD QPR DUVET COVER AND SET SAIL TO CONFRONT BRANSON ON HIS PRIVATE ISLAND IN THE MIDDLE OF THE CARIBBEAN.

THANKS TO THAT CLUELESS COCKNEY I HEADED IN THE WRONG DIRECTION AND DRIFTED AIMLESSLY AROUND THE GLOBE FOR THE NEXT THREE AND A HALF YEARS.

SO TO SURVIVE I HAD TO FASHION WHAT I NEEDED OUT OF SPARE MANNEQUIN PARTS. I CONSTRUCTED A FISHING ROD OUT OF SIX FOREARMS AND A FACE WITH A KNUCKLE IN ITS MOUTH FOR THE REEL.

I MADE A SELECTION OF SERVING BOWLS OUT OF SOME ARSE CHEEKS...

A NUTRIBULLET OUT OF A TOWER OF SKULLS...

AND A TUMBLE DRYER.

AFTER A FEW YEARS AT SEA I BEGAN TO GET LONELY SO I STARTED TO TALK TO THE MANNEQUINS FOR SOME COMPANY.

I HOPE YOU DON'T MIND ME SAYING BUT YOU HAVE A SMASHING BODY.

SOON, DUE TO A COMBINATION OF HEAT EXHAUSTION AND THE CRIPPLING ISOLATION, IN MY MIND THE MANNEQUINS STARTED TO CHAT BACK TO ME AND I BEGAN TO SUSPECT THAT THEY ALL THOUGHT I WAS A DICK.

I THINK JOE'S A DICK.

I AGREE.

IF YOU HAD TO DESCRIBE JOE IN ONE WORD, WHAT WOULD IT BE?

DICK.

AND THANKS TO A FEW BAD EGGS THEY GANGED UP ON ME, STAGED A MUTINY AND MADE ME WALK THE PLANK.

THEN I SPOTTED A LOAD OF FIVERS FLOATING IN THE SEA.

I KNEW THAT MEANT HIS ISLAND WAS NEARBY.
I SWAM TOWARDS LAND FOLLOWING THE FIVERS.

HE WAS COMPLETELY UNFAZED BY ANY OF THIS, WHICH TELLS YOU A LOT ABOUT THE CHARACTER OF THE MAN, AND WHY HE IS WHERE HE IS.

IT SAYS IT HERE ON PAGE 2.

employees must not sniff their co-workers.

OH YEAH, I'M SURPRISED NO ONE ELSE SPOTTED THAT... I GUESS THAT'S WHY YOU GET PAID THE BIG BUCKS.

HE KINDLY LET ME UNWIND AND RECOVER FROM THE SCURVY I'D DEVELOPED WHILE AT SEA. I HAD A FANTASTIC WEEK CHILLING OUT WITH RICHARD.

IS THAT BARACK OBAMA ON A JET SKI?

EVENTUALLY IT WAS TIME FOR ME TO LEAVE AND I WAS THANKING HIM FOR HIS HOSPITALITY WHEN HE HANDED ME A BILL FOR £270,000.

THAT'S HOW MUCH IT COSTS TO STAY ON MY ISLAND FOR A WEEK.

BUT I THOUGHT I WAS STAYING AS YOUR GUEST?

NO. I'M GOING TO USE THE MONEY TO BUY A KEY CUTTER'S IN FROME.

I HAD TO GO BACK TO WORK AT THE MANNEQUIN FACTORY SO I COULD PAY HIM BACK SIXTY QUID A WEEK...

...WHICH HE FLEW OVER TO COLLECT EVERY FRIDAY AT A COST OF £131,000.

BUT I GOT MY OWN BACK COS BRANSON HAD NO IDEA WHAT VIRGIN ACTUALLY MEANT. HE WAS LIVID WHEN I TOLD HIM. SO THAT CHEERED ME UP A BIT.

HARD TIMES

I ALSO HAD A FLATMATE, LYN, WHO NEVER FORGAVE ME FOR NIPPING TO THE SHOPS WHILE SHE WAS ON *WHO WANTS TO BE A MILLIONAIRE.*

HI JOE, IT'S CHRIS TARRANT HERE, I'VE GOT LYN WITH ME, SHE'S UP TO THE ONE MILLION POUND QUESTION, SO THE NEXT VOICE YOU HEAR WILL BE HERS.

HI JOE! I KNOW YOU KNOW THIS ANSWER... JOE? JOE, ARE YOU THERE? IS THIS THE FXXKING ANSWER MACHINE?

PLEASE DON'T SWEAR, YOU'RE ON LIVE TV.

ALL I ASKED YOU TO FXXKING DO JOE IS STAY IN BETWEEN EIGHT AND NINE, YOU FXXKING ARSEHOLE...

RIGHT, GET HER OFF THE SHOW!

ANOTHER SIDE EFFECT OF THE MEDICAL TRIALS WAS THAT I WAS INVISIBLE FOR THE FOLLOWING FORTNIGHT, WHICH RUINED MY HOLIDAY SNAPS.

HERE'S ONE OF ME LOUNGING BY THE POOL.

HERE'S ME DRINKING A SPARKLY COCKTAIL.

HERE'S ME WITH MY ARM ROUND THE WAITER, RAUL.

HERE'S ME FEEDING A HORSE.

HERE'S ME WITH MY HEAD THROUGH ONE OF THOSE FUNNY THINGS.

HERE'S ME DOING A POSE SO IT LOOKS LIKE I'M HOLDING UP THE LEANING TOWER OF PISA.

HERE'S THE MOMENT A SEAGULL LANDED ON MY HEAD.

HERE'S ONE I ACCIDENTALLY TOOK OF MYSELF SITTING ON THE TOILET.

CRIME
DOESN'T PAY

115

MY FIRST KIDNAPPING DIDN'T GO THAT WELL EITHER.

AAAAAAA!!!

THUNK

AAAAAAAAAAAAAAAAAAAAAAAAAAAAAAAAAAAAAAAAAA

I WASN'T A NATURAL BURGLAR EITHER.

HEY.

IT'S ONE MINUTE PAST MIDNIGHT WHICH MEANS IT'S OFFICIALLY YOUR BIRTHDAY!!

HAPPY BIRTHDAY TO YOU! HAPPY BIRTHDAY TO YOU!

SOMEONE'S GROUCHY COS THEY'VE JUST TURNED FORTY.

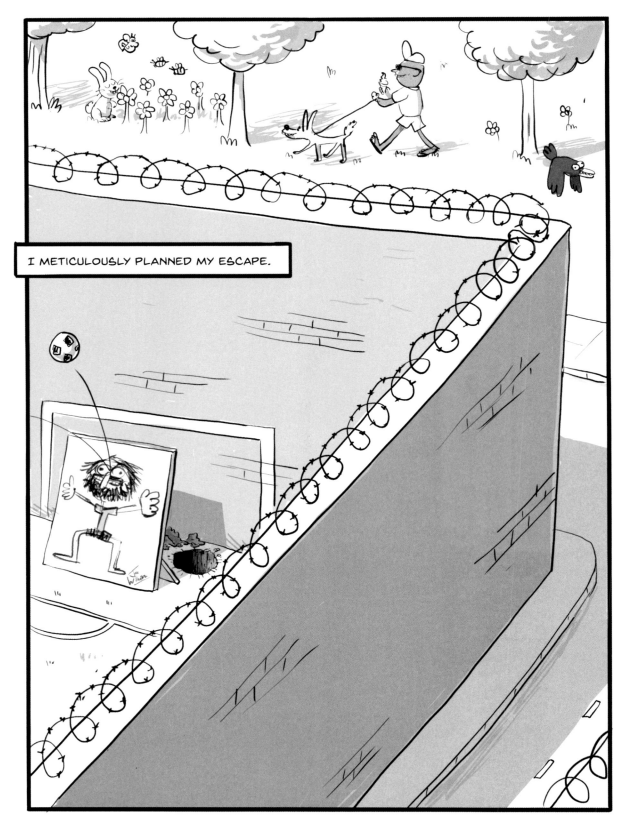

I METICULOUSLY PLANNED MY ESCAPE.

I DIDN'T KNOW WHAT TO SPEND MY MONEY ON NEXT. THEN I STARTED PERSONALIZING EVERYTHING.

I'M BORED OF MY KEY... ANY CHANCE YOU CAN CUT A KEY TO LOOK LIKE ME?

I'LL GIVE IT A GO.

IT DOESN'T LOOK VERY MUCH LIKE ME...

WE'RE QUITE LIMITED WITH WHAT WE CAN DO WITH THESE KEY-CUTTING MACHINES.

IT LOOKS MORE LIKE HIM.

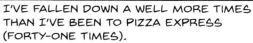

I'VE FALLEN DOWN A WELL MORE TIMES THAN I'VE BEEN TO PIZZA EXPRESS (FORTY-ONE TIMES).

SO I INSTALLED A PAYPHONE DOWN THERE SO I COULD CALL SOMEONE TO PULL ME OUT.

BOLLOCKS, I HAVEN'T GOT ANY CHANGE ON ME.

I WISH I HAD BROADER SHOULDERS.

OH CHEERS... HELLO, I'VE DONE IT AGAIN.

THAT WAS QUICK.

QUITE SOON AFTER CLONING SIXTY-SEVEN VERSIONS OF MYSELF, THE BICKERING STARTED.

WHO'S THE ORIGINAL AGAIN?

NO, I AM.

I AM.

NO, I AM.

NO, I AM.

NO, I AM.

NO, I AM.

NO, I AM.

NO, I...

NO, I AM.

NO, I AM.

NO,

WHERE DID ALL THESE WEAPONS COME FROM?

THE 'ME' THAT'S LEFT ISN'T THE ORIGINAL

WHAT DID I MISS?

BUT WHO CARES? ONLY DIFFERENCE IS NOW I HAVE A MUCH WEAKER BLADDER.

I NEED A PISS AGAIN.

EXPERIENCING
OTHER CULTURES

ON THE PLAINS OF THE SERENGETI I DISCOVERED THAT NOT ALL DARTS ARE TRANQUILLIZER DARTS.

IT'S GOT A PICTURE OF ERIC BRISTOW ON THE FLIGHT.

ARE YOU SURE THAT DART WILL STUN A RHINO?

THERE'S ONLY ONE WAY TO FIND OUT...

THUNK

SAVE THE RHINO

I THINK IT MIGHT BE MY FAULT THAT BIGFOOT WENT INTO HIDING...

WHY ARE YOU CALLED 'BIGFOOT' AND NOT 'BIGFEET'?

IT'S NOT LIKE YOU'VE ONLY GOT ONE BIG FOOT.

HOW BIG ARE YOUR FEET ANYWAY?

MINE ARE A SIZE 10 SO WHAT DOES THAT MAKE YOURS, A SIZE 20?

DO THEY EVEN MAKE SIZE 20 SHOES?

IS THAT WHY YOU WALK ABOUT IN BARE FEET?

I GET MINE FROM SHOE ZONE.

OR RUSSELL AND BROMLEY. WHERE ARE YOU GOING?

I HAVE A TENDENCY TO JUMP TO THE WRONG CONCLUSIONS, ESPECIALLY WHEN I'M UP NORTH.

I FOUND OUT THE WORST TIME TO RUB A MAGIC LAMP IS WHEN YOU HAVE CHRONIC DIARRHOEA.

WHAT ARE YOUR THREE WISHES THEN?

I NEED BOG ROLL.

THERE YOU GO.

WHAT IS YOUR SECOND WISH?

AAAAHHHH, IT'S COMING OUT LIKE HOT LAVA, I NEED MORE BOG ROLL.

FUN FACT FOR YOU: ALIENS ONLY ABDUCT ODDBALLS BECAUSE THEY KNOW NO ONE WILL BELIEVE THEM.

MY ABDUCTION WAS PRETTY STANDARD. THEY SUCKED ME UP OUTSIDE ASDA.

I BLACKED OUT AND WHEN I WOKE UP AN ALIEN HAD ITS FINGER UP MY ARSE.

AFTERWARDS, AS WE WAITED FOR THE RAMP TO LOWER, I DECIDED TO MAKE SOME SMALL TALK.

SO WHAT'S WITH THE WHOLE DIGIT UP THE ARSE THING?

THAT'S WHEN HE WENT VERY COY.

SORRY, I WAS DRUNK. I DON'T KNOW WHY I DID THAT.

AS YOU CAN IMAGINE, I LEFT THE SPACESHIP FUMING.

I ASSUMED IT WAS FOR SCIENTIFIC REASONS!

I WENT STRAIGHT BACK TO ASDA TO COMPLAIN.

CUSTOME
SERVICE

FUNNY HOW IT ALWAYS HAPPENS TO ODDBALLS.

USTOME
SERVICE

GIVING SOMETHING BACK

I TURNED THE GUPTAS' MOOSE INTO A LOVELY LAMP.

I THINK IT BRINGS THE WHOLE ROOM TOGETHER.

I IMAGINED MY IMAGINARY AIR TRAFFIC CONTROLLER BACK AT HIS OLD JOB, BUT I FORGOT TO IMAGINE HIM OFF THE BOOZE.

HE'S JUST REVERSED US INTO TERMINAL 5.

I DONATED A STATUE OF MYSELF TO MY OLD SCHOOL.

I BRIBED THE MANAGER AND GOT CRYSTAL A JOB AT THE LONDON AQUARIUM, BUT BECAUSE SHE'S TOP-HEAVY SHE JUST FLOATED UPSIDE DOWN.

I HAD A PANIC BUTTON INSTALLED IN MY AUNTIE PAM'S HOUSE.

HELLO LOVE, THINGS HAVE GOT OUT OF HAND AGAIN.

I BOUGHT MY EX-FIANCÉE A SOLAR PANEL SO WHEN SHE SEES ME SHE CAN TASER HERSELF WITHOUT CHANGING THE BATTERIES.

I CONCOCTED AN AUDACIOUS PLAN TO BUST MY OLD BURGLARY BUDDY OUT OF PRISON.

I'M IN THE NEXT CELL ALONG. YOU JUST PULLED THE WINDOW OFF THE STATIONERY CUPBOARD.

I WENT BACK AND GAVE THE CLONES I'D SLAUGHTERED A PROPER BURIAL. THE HEADSTONE COST ME A FEW QUID.

The End

ACKNOWLEDGEMENTS

I'D LIKE TO THANK ALL MY ALSATIANS, ESPECIALLY DRAGØR.
I DON'T THINK I'D BE HERE TODAY IF IT WASN'T FOR YOUR CONTINUED
LOVE AND SUPPORT.

I'D ALSO LIKE TO THANK MINTY — YOU'VE HELPED ME MORE THAN YOU
WILL EVER KNOW. FOR LETTING ME BECOME THE MAN I AM TODAY.

I'D ALSO LIKE TO THANK FOXY LADY. I'VE WATCHED YOUR LEADERSHIP
FROM AFAR. YOU ARE THE INSPIRATION AND FOUNDATION FOR THIS BOOK.

I'D ALSO LIKE TO THANK THE ANGLE GRINDER. I'LL NEVER FORGET
OUR TIME IN DELHI.

I'D ALSO LIKE TO THANK RITA. YOU WERE MY EDITOR, MENTOR AND
(HEAVEN HELP YOU) MY BEST FRIEND.

I'D ALSO LIKE TO THANK SUE. IT TAKES A VILLAGE TO RAISE A CHILD.
YOU ARE MY VILLAGE.

I'D ALSO LIKE TO THANK BOB. YOU ENCOURAGED ME TO INDULGE
MYSELF IN MEDIEVAL WEAPONRY. WE SPENT MANY A LONG CAR JOURNEY
CREATING EPIC TALES OF SWORD-WIELDING HEROINES.

I'D ALSO LIKE TO THANK MIKE PATTERSON FOR CHECKING THE
SPELING FOR ME.

I'D ALSO LIKE TO THANK TURPS. THIS BOOK IS THE BRAINCHILD OF A WET
WEDNESDAY AFTERNOON CHAT WE HAD THINKING ABOUT THE STRUGGLES
OF OUR YOUNGER SELVES AND LOOKING FORWARD TO HELPING
GENERATIONS OF YOUNG DOG OWNERS STILL TO COME.

I'D ALSO LIKE TO THANK BATTERY ACID FOR YOUR HONESTY, PATIENCE
AND BRAVERY. EVERYTHING GOOD IN MY LIFE IS BECAUSE OF YOUR
LOVE AND CARE.

I'D ALSO LIKE TO THANK BIG VAL FOR REGULARLY REJECTING MY FIRST IDEAS THUS FORCING ME INTO DEEPER THOUGHT.

I'D ALSO LIKE TO THANK MERTHYR TYDFIL. NEW WRITERS WILL STUDY YOU LONG AFTER YOU ARE NO LONGER WITH US.

I'D ALSO LIKE TO THANK LUCIFER FOR EMPOWERING ME AND SO MANY OTHERS WITH YOUR GREATNESS.

I'D ALSO LIKE TO THANK GUNPOWDER FOR GUIDING ME THROUGH THE PROCESS OF HOW TO BE A NON-AWARD-WINNING WRITER.

I'D ALSO LIKE TO THANK BERNIE NOLAN AND HER RESEARCH TEAM. WITHOUT YOU THERE IS NO BOOK.

I'D ALSO LIKE TO THANK DASHER. YOU TAUGHT ME THAT DESPITE WHAT WE CONSIDER CONVINCING THEORETICAL AND EMPIRICAL EVIDENCE, A CYCLE TIME-BASED ACCOUNT IS LESS VALID THAN A PREFERRED ACTIVATION AND MICRO-LAPSES THEORY.

I'D ALSO LIKE TO THANK COURTNEY. I WROTE THIS FOR YOU BUT WHEN I BEGAN IT I HAD NOT REALIZED THAT ALSATIANS GROW QUICKER THAN BOOKS.

I'D ALSO LIKE TO THANK THE MUSCLES FROM BRUSSELS. YOU STUCK WITH ME THROUGH THIS WHOLE EPIC ROLLERCOASTER. I WOULDN'T TRADE YOU FOR ALL THE GLITTER IN THE WORLD.

SOURCES

WELCOME TO WEAVING: THE MODERN GUIDE BY LINDSEY CAMPBELL

HANDWEAVER'S PATTERN BOOK: THE ESSENTIAL ILLUSTRATED GUIDE TO OVER 600 FABRIC WEAVES BY ANNE DIXON

WEAVING AN OTHERWISE: IN-RELATIONS METHODOLOGICAL PRACTICE EDITED BY AMANDA R. TACHINE AND Z. NICOLAZZO

LEARNING TO WEAVE BY DEBORAH CHANDLER

A HANDBOOK OF WEAVES: 1875 ILLUSTRATIONS BY G. H. OELSNER

THREADS OF LIFE: A HISTORY OF THE WORLD THROUGH THE EYE OF A NEEDLE BY CLARE HUNTER

PERTH: ITS WEAVERS AND WEAVING AND THE WEAVER INCORPORATION OF PERTH BY PETER BAXTER

WEAVING AS AN ART FORM: A PERSONAL STATEMENT BY THEO MOORMAN

THE COMPLETE BASKET-MAKING BOOK WEAVING TECHNICAL WITH NATURAL MATERIAL BY REIKO SASAKI

ABOUT THE AUTHOR

JOE WILKINSON IS A REGULAR FIGURE ON KENT'S SUNDAY MORNING CAR BOOT SALE SCENE, BOTH AS A VENDOR AND A PATRON. HE'S RIDDEN SEVERAL BICYCLES AND CAN PUT HIS FIST IN HIS MOUTH. HE'S NEVER OWNED, READ OR WRITTEN A BOOK IN HIS LIFE.

HE IS ALSO AN AWARD-WINNING COMEDIAN AND HAS BEEN A FIXTURE ON OUR TELEVISION SCREENS FOR OVER A DECADE. MAKING REGULAR APPEARANCES ON SHOWS SUCH AS *8 OUT OF 10 CATS DOES COUNTDOWN, HAVE I GOT NEWS FOR YOU* AND *NEVER MIND THE BUZZCOCKS*, HE IS REGARDED AS ONE OF THE FINEST AND MOST SURREAL COMEDIANS ON THE CIRCUIT.

AS AN ACTOR, HE HAS STARRED IN HIT SHOWS SUCH AS *HIM & HER, MIRANDA, DEREK, AFTERLIFE, SEX EDUCATION, THE COCKFIELDS* AND *ROVERS*.

ABOUT THE ILLUSTRATOR

HENRY PAKER IS AN AWARD-WINNING COMEDIAN, WRITER AND ILLUSTRATOR. HE CO-WRITES AND STARS IN THE BBC RADIO 4 SITCOM *REINCARNATHAN* AND THE SKETCH SHOW *SMALL SCENES*. HE IS CO-HOST OF THE *THREE BEAN SALAD* PODCAST.

HE ILLUSTRATES ADAM KAY'S CHILDREN'S BOOKS, INCLUDING THE SUNDAY TIMES BESTSELLER *KAY'S MARVELLOUS MEDICINE* AND *KAY'S BRILLIANT BRAINS* FOR *WORLD BOOK DAY*. THEY HAVE ALSO JUST COLLABORATED ON THEIR FIRST PICTURE BOOK, *AMY GETS EATEN*. HENRY HAS ILLUSTRATED TWO HUMOUR BOOKS, *WHY STEVE WAS LATE* AND *DON'T ARM WRESTLE A PIRATE*.

HENRY SPLITS HIS TIME BETWEEN BEING AWAKE AND BEING ASLEEP.

BLOOPERS

I USED TO LIVE OVER THE HILL FROM THE WORLD'S ONLY RUDE FELL WALKER.

MORNING!

I LIKE YOUR NEW SCARF.

181